CW00728250

Numerology

A Beginner's Guide to the Mysteries of Numerology

Lauren Lingard

Table of Contents

Introduction

Numbers are everywhere. Not just the numbers we can see, like those on our clocks and phone screens—or on the cash register as we check out at the store—but hidden numbers. The mathematics behind everything that is physically and chemically extant. Through mathematics and geometry, numbers tell the story of everything that surrounds us. Numerologists believe that numbers are the most basic building block of the universe—a vast and complex system. Behind even the atom, the electron, or the proton, there are numbers; numbers that, through their unique vibrational frequencies, inform every aspect of creation, right down to your very own life.

A shroud of mystery surrounds the art and science of numerology, the ancient practice of divining by numbers. If you have ever wondered "What is numerology?" or "What does 11:11 mean?" or; if you have found yourself drawn over and over again to certain numbers that reappear throughout your life, numerology may be for you.

This book aims to help you, the beginner, decode the mysteries of numerology, enabling you to use this ancient wisdom to better understand and improve your own self. This book will discuss the history of numerology; how numerology works and which numbers you will want to calculate; the meanings of some of the most important numbers you will encounter; and step-by-step instructions on how to practice basic numerology for yourself.

The ancient art of numerology promises to help you find your true purpose in life, improve your existing relationships and build strong, new ties. It will also help to guide you toward the best decisions you can make for yourself in your personal life and professional life. These and many more benefits of numerology are available for you to apply to your own life if you are willing, and ready, to dig in and discover what this ancient science has to offer you.

Chapter One: What is Numerology?

Put simply, numerology is an ancient system of divination based on numbers. Numerology is to numbers as astrology is to stars; like the signs of the Zodiac, numbers—the most basic building blocks of the universe—influence us all profoundly from the time of our birth. Numerologists believe that understanding how we relate to these numbers and harnessing their power can help us to better ourselves and the world around us. Numerologists study the vibrational frequency or energy of numbers to decipher what their most spiritual meanings are.

Numerologists use numerology charts much like astrologists create astrological or birth charts. These charts contain much wisdom and insight about an individual calculated by that person's full name and date of birth. A numerology chart includes multiple numbers that are calculated in different ways to provide different types of guidance and answers.

There are actually many different numerological beliefs and practices around the world, though in this book, we will focus primarily on a modern take on Pythagorean numerology. We will briefly explore other numerological practices around the world in the next chapter: *The History of Numerology*.

Numerology is not the same thing as mathematics, although the two are related. The mathematics involved in calculating numerological numbers is very simple addition and subtraction. You do not need to have aced calculus class to understand and use numerology! You only need a basic understanding of how to add numbers together (or a calculator). In the following sections, you will learn how these simple calculations are performed.

Types of Numerology

There are three major types of numerology, each one having originated in a different part of the world, as we will explore in the next chapter. No one type of numerology is better than the others, and they can actually be used together in a numerology reading—though this is not recommended for beginners, as mixing the different systems can get confusing.

The three major types of numerology are Kabbalah numerology, Chaldean numerology, and Pythagorean numerology.

Kabbalah numerology has its origins in Hebrew mysticism. This system of numerology is based on the sacred number of 22, which is also the number of Major Arcana cards in the Tarot. Kabbalah numerology places a great focus on letters and is thus most often used to divine meaning from birth names.

Chaldean numerology originated in ancient Mesopotamia. This is also where astrology originated, and Chaldean numerology has close ties to astrology. In Chaldean numerology, the single digit numbers 1-8 have unique vibrations, and each letter in the alphabet is assigned to one. The number 9, however, is kept sacred and separate in Chaldean numerology.

Pythagorean numerology is the most common type of numerology seen in the western world today, and therefore it is the system of numerology we will focus on in this book. Pythagoras, the Greek philosopher and mathematician, is credited with inventing this numerological system in the 6th century BC. Pythagorean numerology, like Chaldean numerology, says that each single digit number has a unique vibrational frequency. However, in Pythagorean numerology, all single digit numbers 1-9 are used. Pythagorean numerology, as we will see in depth later in this book, also venerates certain double-digit numbers, including 11, 22, and 33. You will learn more about the history of Pythagorean numerology in the next chapter.

How does numerology work?

In Pythagorean numerology, which is the type of numerology we will focus on in the rest of this book, each number 1-9 is said to have an innate cosmic meaning that includes personality traits, both positive and negative. Each letter of the alphabet is also said to correspond to a number 1-9:

1. A, J, S
2. B, K, T
3. C, L, U
4. D, M, V
5. E, N, W
6. F, O, X
7. G, P, Y
8. H, Q, Z
9. I, R

The basic practice of numerology is then to convert each individual letter that makes up a word into its corresponding number. Those numbers are then summed, or added, together. If the sum total is a two-digit number or higher (but not 11, 22, or 33—more on that later), the individual digits are summed again until you are left with a number 1-9.

This may sound complicated, but it's actually quite simple! Let's take a look at a couple of examples. For instance, the name Katherine:

K = 2, A = 1, T = 2, H = 8, E = 5, R = 9, I = 9, N = 5, E = 5

So:

K+A+T+H+E+R+I+N+E = 2+1+2+8+5+9+9+5+5 = 46 = 4+6 = 10 = 1+0 = 1

The number that ultimately corresponds to the name Katherine is 1.

However, to fully understand what numerology has to say about you as a person, you will need to calculate numbers for much more than just your first name. We will go into a great deal more depth about the various numbers you can calculate for yourself, and why you should calculate them, in future chapters.

Let's look at another example. For instance, a date. Let's say, the year 2020:

$2 + 0 + 2 + 0 = 4$

So, the number that corresponds to 2020 is 4.

You can see that at its core, numerological calculations are actually quite simple and easy to understand! They are calculations you can do yourself, if you are patient. Though, many, both free and paid, online calculators are available to do the work for you.

But as you will discover throughout this book, there is much more to numerology than just these calculations. For one, calculating your numerology chart requires knowing how to perform multiple simple calculations like these to get all your Core Numbers; we will go over this in depth later in the book. What is most important, and what requires study and expertise, is the interpretation of these Core Numbers in your numerology chart, applying the calculations to your life and deciphering what they mean in specific instances so you can reap the benefits of numerological knowledge.

Core Numbers

In Pythagorean, or western, numerology, a full numerological chart comprises multiple numbers that are come to by calculations like the examples above. We will go into further detail on these calculations later in the book so that you can make your very own numerological chart.

There are many potential numbers to calculate in numerology, but five of these numbers are considered to make up the most important building blocks of the self. Numerologists call these numbers Core Numbers. The five core numbers in western numerology are:

- The Life Path Number
- The Destiny Number (sometimes called the Expression Number)
- The Soul Urge Number (sometimes called the Soul Number or the Heart's Desire Number)
- The Personality Number
- The Birth Day Number

This book dedicates a chapter to exploring each one of these Core Numbers in detail. First, however, we will look back through the ages to the history of numerology and study what each individual digit means independent of its place in your numerological chart.

Chapter Two: The History of Numerology

Numerology has existed for as long as human beings have recognized and used numbers. Numerology practices, if we take a broad definition of the term, are culturally and/or religiously significant in many parts of the world. For example, the Chinese sacred text, the I Ching, assigns spiritual values to numbers, and, thus, can be said to include numerological concepts. Ancient numerological beliefs and practices have been recorded in China, Japan, India, Europe, the Middle East, and elsewhere. The sacred meanings of numbers seem then to be intrinsic to human culture, having popped up consistently around the globe, often independently of one another.

As you learned in the previous chapter, the three major types of numerology originated in different parts of the world; however, their histories are connected. While Pythagoras may be the father of western numerology, his ideas were heavily influenced by his study of Chaldean numerology. So, it is with Chaldean numerology that we begin our historical study.

The Ancient Babylonians

Mesopotamia, known as the cradle of civilization, is the birthplace for so much ancient knowledge, including mathematics, astronomy, astrology, and numerology. It was the ancient Sumerians as far back as 3200 BC who first developed the numerical system on which later Mesopotamian mathematics and numerology were based.

The name Chaldean numerology comes from the Chaldean people, who believed that their ancestry was not altogether human, but divine. These people took over the ancient city of Babylon that later grew into the Babylonian Empire, which was finally known as the Chaldean Empire before its fall to Persia. But, Chaldean numerology predates Chaldean rule of Mesopotamia; the name is a bit of a misnomer.

To the ancient Mesopotamian people, the numbers 1-8 held sacred meaning, with number 9 being the most sacred of all. Double digit numbers were believed to represent a person's inner life, while the single digit numbers were said to represent who a person was outwardly. It was believed in Chaldean numerology that a person's name and birthday should always be in harmony, and since birth dates cannot be changed, a great deal of importance was placed on choosing the correct name for a person at birth.

When Alexander the Great conquered Mesopotamia, he brought back to Egypt, with him, considerable knowledge from the advanced Chaldean people. It was here that Pythagoras learned of Chaldean numerology, which he studied for many years and eventually adapted into his own system, the system of numerology we use in the western world today.

Pythagoras

Pythagoras was a venerated mathematician and philosopher in ancient Greece whose name is still known across the world today. He is best known for his huge contribution to the study of geometry—what is still known today as the Pythagorean theorem, which calculates the hypotenuse of a right triangle. For this, Pythagoras is known as the father of geometry, but he is also known as the father of modern numerology.

Pythagoras not only studied Chaldean numerology and mathematics for 22 years in Egypt, but he is said to have actually been captured and taken to Babylon. While a captive in Babylon, Pythagoras studied with a Zoroastrian priest and learned about the innate harmony of the universe. It was then that Pythagoras discovered the relationship between music and numbers, which helped him to make his breakthroughs in developing his own numerological system based on the Chaldean.

Pythagoras is said to have stated famously that the world is built on the power of numbers. He believed that all phenomena in the universe could be expressed as numbers, and that these numbers correspond to universal vibrations. Pythagoras discovered that by pairing each letter of the alphabet with its corresponding single digit number, he could calculate what he and other Greek philosophers believed to be the true divinatory meaning of any written word. This especially included names and birthdays.

Unfortunately, Pythagoras's teachings were not written down, and the only way we know of what Pythagoras taught is through the writings of his students.

The Dark Ages and Resurgence

Numerology fell out of favor, along with astrology and other newly labeled occult practices as the Church rose to power. After the First Council of Nicea in 325 AD, the Christian church outright banned numerology throughout the Roman Empire as a civil violation to practice.

Throughout the dark ages, numerology and other occult arts were hidden and repressed; though it is also worth noting that some medieval practices involved sacred numbers in the Bible. Numbers 3 and 7 are said to be especially significant in the Christian mythos, and 666 is considered to be the mark of the beast.

It wasn't until the late 19th and early 20th centuries that numerology, as we know it today, came into popularity. Partly responsible for this was Count Louis Hamon of England, also known by his stage name or pseudonym Cheiro. Cheiro was a fortune teller who served the rich and famous of London.

It is Mrs. L. Dow Balliett, however, who is credited with first bringing Pythagoras's theories together with Christian numerological influences to create the beginnings of the western numerological system we know today. Balliett did so around the start of the 20th century, and her student Juno Jordan continued her work, going on to publish a book called "The Romance in Your Name" in 1965. The new age movement in the 1970s, and onward, helped propel the popularity of Jordan's work. This book first laid out many of the numerological calculations still used today. Other authors have since taken up the subject and built upon it, but Balliet and Jordan were truly the first modern day numerologists.

Chapter Three: Single Digit Numbers

In Pythagorean or western numerology, as you learned earlier in this book, each number 1-9 has its own divine energy and corresponds to a specific set of characteristics, both positive and negative—almost like each number has its own unique personality. In this chapter, we will look, in depth, at the meanings behind each one of these profound, cosmic numbers and decipher their hidden powers.

In later chapters, we will look at how you can apply these number personalities to your life, using various numerological calculations to find specific numbers in your numerology chart; the combination of which is unique to you and your life. Understanding what each one of these numbers represents lays the foundation for deciphering their full, complex, relational meaning in your numerology chart.

Number 0

The number 0 will not show up in the Core Numbers of your numerology chart, but it is nonetheless an important number to learn about in numerology. The 0 represents infinity and energetically includes all things, as well as all possible potential. Thus, the number 0 signifies possibility.

Number 1

The number 1 in numerology (the first number) represents new beginnings, opportunities, and momentum. Like Aries is the first sign in the Zodiac, the number 1, in numerology, is all about moving forward, like the horns of the ram. Spiritually, the number 1 represents the very birth of the divine universe.

Number 1 personality types are incredibly independent with a strong urge to protect others. They are goal-oriented and innovative. On the flip side, though, number 1's negative traits are that they can be forceful, risky, and doubtful. These individuals need to learn to work with others without losing their individuality. Number 1's are in danger of becoming self-absorbed and emphasizing their own needs over others. These people would do well to remember that no man is an island, and friends and family are here to help.

Number 2

The number 2 in numerology represents partnership and harmony. It is considered a very feminine number linked to intuition and psychic ability. The number 2 serves as a mediator and peacemaker, bringing balance with it.

Number 2 personality types are followers rather than leaders. They are so good at peacemaking that number 2's are compatible with all other numbers; this personality type makes an excellent partner, husband, or wife. They are supremely intuitive, unifying, and influential; but on their darker side, they are also indecisive, overly sensitive, and unassertive. Number 2's need to be careful not to become too self-effacing.

Number 3

The number 3 in numerology represents creative expression and communication. It is a number that dances through life; a social butterfly, and a very creative, artistic soul. The number 3 spiritually represents the contribution of two joined forces, making it the very definition of creation!

Number 3 personality types are all about the joy of being alive! Their work inspires everyone it touches. These individuals are communicative, charming, and artistic, but can also be naive, unfocused, and shallow. Number 3s need to be careful not to be superficial, and they can be known to act moody.

Number 4

The number 4 in numerology represents stability and dependability. Like the earth beneath your feet, the number 4 is strong, sure and true; a number you can always count on.

Number 4 personality types are the builders of the world, because they start with such a strong, dependable foundation. These individuals can get the job at hand done and do it right every time. They are practical, loyal, and service-oriented, but they can also be dull, rigid, and even dogmatic. Number 4 types should take care not to become too distant from others.

Number 5

The number 5 in numerology represents freedom and adventure. A pro at change, 5 is highly adaptable and able to go with the flow. Number 5 is never one to stagnate, preferring to move on to the next great thing. A great way to conceptualize the number 5 is to think of the 5 senses.

Number 5 personality types love to travel and meet new people; they are keenly aware of the diversity of life, which makes them unprejudiced toward others who are different from them. Number 5 types are curious, adaptable, and sociable, but they can also be unreliable, directionless, and noncommittal. These individuals should be careful not to become too self-indulgent.

Number 6

The number 6 in numerology represents unconditional love, symbolizing the heart. The love of the number 6 is a powerful force for healing and nurturing. This number has a soft, tender, and caring spirit.

Number 6 personality types are the ones that we all go to when we need support and help. These individuals serve others happily and selflessly. They are supremely supportive, protective, and romantic; but on the darker side, they can also be passive, self-sacrificing, and idealistic, and they should be careful not to allow themselves to take on tyrannical traits if their "mothering" goes a few steps too far.

Number 7

The number 7 represents digging deeper. It is spiritually a very special number as it aligns with the seven planets, the seven days of the week, and seven notes of music on the musical scale. The 7 is a very wise and spiritual number, but it leads with its head, not its heart.

Number 7 personality types are spiritual, curious, and analytical, but on the flip side, they can also be reclusive, secretive, and suspicious. These individuals have the ability to probe the deep mysteries of the universe and discover the hidden spiritual truths. But number 7's need to be careful to avoid withdrawing from others and into their own worlds too much. Number 7's can also be perfectionists, to their detriment.

Number 8

The number 8 represents achievement, material wealth, and success, so much so that some followers of numerology have even changed their names in order to get more number 8's in their numerology charts!

Number 8 personality types are the practical people of the world. They are ambitious, generous, and determined, but they can also have the negative traits of being materialistic, authoritative, and entitled. Number 8 is the number associated with large organizations and corporations, and as such, these individuals would be wise to avoid becoming demanding. Numbers 8's should strive to use their powers for good and remember to work towards the good of the many rather than concentrate on accumulating wealth for oneself.

Number 9

The number 9 has the energy of completion; in contrast to its counterpart number 1, the beginning, number 9 represents the end. But it is not a final end that 9 represents, rather the end of one journey and the possibilities of the next! Number 9 is an old soul, having been through it all.

Number 9 personality types are the humanitarians among us. They are awakened, talented, and supportive, but they can also be resentful, self-sacrificing, and self-pitying. Number 9 types should take care not to become egocentric and make an effort to ground and anchor themselves.

Chapter Four: Master Numbers

You have already learned that in numerology, most numbers are summed as individual digits until a single digit is eventually reached, breaking down numbers into their most essential forms, called root numbers. But what about those few, special multi-digit numbers that do not get broken down into single digits? These are supremely powerful and divine numbers whose meaning we must pay close attention to. These special numbers, that numerologists do not break down, are called Master Numbers.

The Master Numbers are 11, 22, and 33. Any time you are calculating a numerological chart, you should stop if your digits sum to one of these three Master Numbers; do not break them down to their roots. For example, you do not add 2 and 2 together, but read them as 22, whereas 44 is read as 4+4 = 8.

Master Numbers 11, 22, and 33 vibrate at a higher frequency than do other numbers and together make up what numerologist's call the Triangle of Enlightenment. So, 44, while it is a powerful number, is not a Master Number, because 4 is not part of the triangle. It is not the doubling of the numbers that makes a Master Number, but rather the specific doubled number itself, 1, 2, or 3.

Together, these numbers can be conceived of as the stages of a great spiritual project: 11 means envisioning, 22 means using practical means to build on that vision, and 33 means sharing that vision with the world.

So, the Master Numbers carry with them a "master" potential, but this power does come at a price: If you see Master Numbers in your chart, you are likely to suffer many setbacks and injustices in life on your way to this mastery. Tapping into the positive energies and the powerful potential of these numbers can be challenging because these personality types can be hard to handle. The life paths of master visionaries, master builders, and master teachers are not easy to follow, but the benefits are worth the struggle, as the creative process laid out by the Master Numbers leads to transformative results.

In this chapter, we will take a look at each one of the Master Numbers in depth to uncover the wisdom that the Triangle of Enlightenment has to teach us. We will cover Power Numbers and Angel Numbers, which are other types of multiple digit numbers, in the next two chapters.

Master Number 11

Number 11 is the first Master Number and the number that represents dreamers and visionaries. Number 11 is said to represent a stronger version of its root number, which is 2. (That is, if you were to continue to sum the individual digits, you would get 2: $1+1 = 2$) As such, number 11 vibrates with a profoundly intuitive and psychic energy and has immense healing and nurturing capabilities.

But the number 11 also includes double the number 1, and thus connotes an intensified version of number 1 energy, which is masculine and action oriented. So, within Master Number 11, there is both the ultimate feminine and ultimate masculine energy; in Pythagoras's mind, it is the merging of the king and queen of the Greek Gods, Zeus and Hera.

This is perhaps the most psychic of all numbers studied in numerology. Master Number 11 truly represents the human potential to surpass the mundane and achieve complete spiritual enlightenment. It also represents the duality of man and divinity; of darkness and light; ignorance and illumination. As such, the number 11 walks a thin line between self-destruction and visionary greatness.

Master Number 11 personality types are extremely intuitive and inventive, but also imbued with charisma and leadership. They have a profound destiny to reveal something significant to the world as a divine messenger or revelator. But Number 11's need to be careful not to cultivate fear and build up phobias, as tends to happen when their energies are turned inward rather than focused on the greater good of the world.

Master Number 22

Master Number 22 is a very powerful number that represents practical idealism and the progress of humankind as a whole. Number 22 is all about growth and expansion, working for the good of the many rather than the few.

This Master Number is said to be a stronger version of its root number, which is 4 (2+2 = 4). As such, number 22 takes the stable, earthy, practical energy of the 4 and amplifies it. But number 22 also represents an amplified version of the number 2 vibrational frequency, which is all about intuition and nurturing. You can see then why Master Number 22 is called the Master Builder: It has the capacity to take the dreams of the number 2 and bring them into reality with its strong number 4 energy.

Master Number 22 personality types have a divine destiny to be the builders of this world, but if number 22's shy away from their ambition and responsibility, they risk wasting their potential and becoming destructively self-critical.

Master Number 33

Master Number 33 is sometimes left out depending on which sources you are using to study numerology. Sometimes only 11 and 22 are considered to be Master Numbers, but for the sake of completeness, we will study number 33 as well.

This Master Number is supremely rare to come up in the core numbers of a numerological chart. This is because the only way to get a number 33 as your Destiny Number is to have a first, middle, and last name which each sum to 11 when their individual digits are added. To have a number 33 as your Life Path Number is also very rare, as it requires that either all three parts of your date of birth are 11s or that the year, at least, sums to 22. There were only 7 years in the 20th century that sum up to Master Number 22, so you can see that by the math, Master Number 33 is rare indeed.

Master Number 33 combines numbers 11 and 22, taking them beyond their full potential. As such, it is the most spiritually evolved of all numbers; the top point on the Triangle of Enlightenment.

Master Number 33 is called the Master Teacher. This personality type lacks its own ambition, instead giving its all to uplift humanity spiritually. This number has a divine destiny to share its enlightenment with the world.

Chapter Five: Power Numbers

Power Numbers are any double-digit numbers that are not 11, 22, or 33—that is, their individual digits do not appear in the Triangle of Enlightenment. Power Numbers like 44, 55, and so forth are not Master Numbers, but as their name implies, they are indeed powerful numbers.

The presence of duplicate digits intensifies the influence of these numbers and makes the energy attributes of each amplified. But there is another layer to these numbers, which is the single digit Root Number to which they sum. This Root Number influences the vibrational frequency of the Power Number; so that 88, for example, does not only connote the double energy of the 8's but also the energy of the 7 to which it ultimately sums. (8+8 = 16 = 1+6 = 7)

These Power Numbers should not appear in your Core Numbers within your numerological chart. If you did calculate a Power Number for one of your Core Numbers, you would simply sum the two digits to break it down to its Root Number. (For instance, 55 = 5+5 = 10 = 1+0 = 1)

But professional numerologists take these Power Numbers into account when they create your numerological chart. For example, if your Life Path Number is 8 summed from 44, this creates a slightly different energy than an 8 that was summed from 35. These advanced numerology practices will not be covered in depth within this book, but a description of what each Power Number represents is given here:

Power Number 44

(44 = 4+4 = 8)

Power Number 44 represents doubled energy of the number 4, which is extremely dependable, organized, and practical. This creates an excellent foundation for a thriving number 8, which is all about success and prosperity. Power Number 44 is therefore a real go-getter of a number and can accomplish much, with a huge potential for success in business.

Power Number 55

$(55 = 5+5 = 10 = 1+0 = 1)$

Power Number 55 is a textbook disrupter in the greatest sense. The double 5's represent a huge amount of freedom and adventure. Meanwhile, the 1 to which they sum is all about leadership and new beginnings. This sets up the Power Number 55 to have extreme ambition and drive and to be leaders who break new and exciting ground!

Power Number 66

$(66 = 6+6 = 12 = 1+2 = 3)$

This Power Number is the most verbally communicative of all numbers and represents the greatest height of human artistic endeavor. The 3 here brings creativity and joy to the double 6's sense of responsibility and service. Power Number 66 then has potential to be a hugely inspirational force.

Power Number 77

$(77 = 7+7 = 14 = 1+4 = 5)$

The Power Number 77 represents the interesting combination of the serious, introspective, spiritual 7's with the adventurous nature of the

5. Power Number 77 is an outside-the-box thinker with the potential to reach the pinnacle of human spiritual thought!

Power Number 77 also involves in its root calculation the Karmic Lesson Number 14, which you will learn about in the next chapter.

Power Number 88

(88 = 8+8 = 16 = 1+6 = 7)

Power Number 88 is a number of great spiritual potential. The double energy of the 8's makes a visionary power that transforms into the most spiritual of the single digit numbers: the 7. Like Power Number 77, Power Number 88 carries the potential to reach the pinnacle of spiritualism.

Power Number 88 also involves in its root calculation the 'Karmic Lesson Number 16', which you will learn about in the next chapter.

Power Number 99

(99 = 9+9 = 18 = 1+8 = 9)

The final Power Number, number 99, represents the ultimate humanitarian. Not only does this Power Number resonate with the power of double 9's, but the numbers sum in root to 9 as well. So here we have 3 number 9's, a very magical number. Power Number 99 has the potential to make the world a truly better place.

Chapter Six: Karmic Lesson Numbers

Karmic Lesson Numbers, also called Karmic Debt Numbers or simply Karmic Numbers, are based on the ancient belief in reincarnation. In numerology, we are said to go through many iterations of life, and during these lifetimes we can acquire karma or karmic debt.

When a Karmic Lesson Number shows up in a calculation on your numerological chart, this indicates a weak area of yourself and something that you should be working on to improve. It is a lesson you are here to learn in this lifetime, based off of the karma of your psychic past.

Like Power Numbers, Karmic Lesson Numbers should not appear in your Core Numbers within your numerological chart. If you did calculate a Karmic Lesson Number for one of your Core Numbers, you would simply sum the two digits to break it down to its Root Number. But do make note of any Karmic Lesson Numbers that come up in your calculations. These Karmic Debt Numbers influence your Core Numbers in advanced numerology practices.

Karmic Lesson Number 13

Karmic Lesson Number 13 represents many obstacles in the way of one's hard work. This Karmic Lesson Number is all about burden and the desire one may have to give in and quit when the going gets tough. Karmic Lesson Number 13 says to itself that its goals were impossible in the first place and could never be attained.

To overcome this karmic debt, the 13 should be mindful not to become lazy or get overly negative minded. The solution is to focus the energy of Karmic Number 13 towards a single goal and stick with it no matter what comes your way.

There is a temptation with Karmic Lesson Number 13 to take shortcuts in order to lighten the burden this number carries, but this is inadvisable. Instead, if number 13's show up in your Core Number calculations, take care to stay focused and organized in your life and especially in your work. Success is not out of reach!

Karmic Lesson Number 14

Karmic Lesson Number 14 represents a constant stream of change, so much so that a person with this Karmic Debt Number will be forced to adapt over and over again to unforeseen circumstances.

To overcome this karmic debt, the 14 must focus on moderation and modesty. There is a grave possibility here of turning to substance abuse and hedonism if Karmic Lesson 14 is not worked on and improved. It is also important for 14 to maintain some sense of order during the characteristic ups and downs to which it must adapt and keep focused on their true dreams in spite of the obstacles they may face.

Karmic Lesson Number 16

Karmic Lesson Number 16 represents the death of one's ego. It is all about destruction of the old and rebirth as new. The loss of one's ego is often a painful and difficult process because during life, most of us spend time building up and inflating our egos as survival mechanisms. As challenging as it may be, on the other side of Karmic Lesson Number 16 lies spiritual rebirth.

The humility that results from the destruction of the ego brings with it the potential for powerful rebirth and good. The 16 is in danger, though, of using its intuition and intellect to judge others and thus cycle back into egoism.

Karmic Lesson Number 19

Karmic Lesson Number 19 teaches us that no man or woman is an island; we cannot go it alone all of the time. This Karmic Lesson Number is about independence, but that independence can easily be taken too far. Oftentimes this independence is by choice, as the number 19 does not want to listen to or work with others.

The number 19 needs to lean into interconnectivity and interdependence in order to heal from this karmic debt. In doing so, there is potential here for great love, friendship, and support.

Chapter Seven: Angel Numbers

Angel numbers are similar to Master Numbers, but for one major difference: They do not show up in your numerology chart. When calculating a numerology chart, you will always break down Angel Numbers by summing their individual digits.

The magic of Angel Numbers instead is outside of your numerology chart, in your everyday life. These are the three, four, or more digit repeating numbers that may seem to follow you everywhere: 11:11 on the clock, $11.11 at the checkout counter, and so on and so forth. Angel Numbers are believed to be divine guidance and a sign that you are on the right path. It is said that Angel Numbers are the way angels communicate with us.

In general, when you see repeating Angel Numbers popping up in your life, it is a sign that someone is watching and encouraging you. Each Angel Number also has its own specific meaning. We will go over some of the most common angel numbers below.

Angel Number 111

This Angel Number 111 is all about you and your destiny. This is a sign from the heavens that it is time to start manifesting your dreams and making your goals a reality. But in order to manifest the good, we need to cast aside what is holding us back. Take 111 as a sign to examine your shadow self and cut ties with that which no longer serves you.

Angel Number 222

While the number 2 represents harmony and balance, the number 222 actually tells you that something is out of balance: either in your emotional life, your physical self, or in your mind. Are you working too much and not taking care of yourself? Take 222 as a sign to find balance and moderation in your life.

Angel Number 333

This Angel Number is a deeply spiritual one. It is a calling to rise up and accomplish your ultimate life purpose. You have unique gifts and the opportunity to make an impact on the world. Take 333 as a sign that it's time to tap into your own potential and use those gifts.

Angel Number 444

This Angel Number is a symbol of hope and positivity. Angel Number 444 is the angels' way of telling you that you're on the right track and to keep moving forward. If you are seeing this number in your life, likely you are in the midst of a struggle or working hard towards a goal. Take 444 as a sign that you have almost reached the next level.

Angel Number 555

This Angel Number is an omen of coming change. Perhaps you are feeling like you have plateaued in your professional life, or that you are stuck in a personal situation you cannot get out of. Take 555 as a positive sign that change is coming your way, but it will not happen if you do not work for it: Take this opportunity to take the next step and bring your positive change underway!

Angel Number 666

Despite the bad reputation this number picked up from the Church, Angel Number 666 is not all about evil and demons. In fact, when you see this Angel Number in your life, it is a symbol of the internal battles you are facing. Take Angel Number 666 as a sign to stop and take control of your negative thoughts, before they take control of you.

Angel Number 777

This Angel Number is a very spiritual one. When Angel Number 777 appears in your life, it is either a sign of a big spiritual awakening to come or a sign from the angels that you are in alignment with your divine purpose. Take Angel Number 777 as a sign to allow yourself to blossom and open up to all the gifts the universe has to offer you.

Angel Number 888

This Angel Number is a surefire sign that abundant blessings are on their way to you. The angels and other divine powers will shower you with spiritual abundance, financial wealth, or physical good health. But do not forget that you still have to put in the work to make your dreams happen. Take Angel Number 888 as a sign that the path you are on will lead you to success if you keep at it.

Angel Number 999

This Angel Number represents the end of something, as 9 is the last single digit. Sometimes, endings can be sad events, but every ending comes with the opportunity for a new beginning. When Angel Number 999 appears in your life, take it as a sign to think positively of whatever in your life is coming to an end, and look forward to the next cycle in your life.

Angel Number 1010

This Angel Number represents spiritual development and growth. When you see Angel Number 1010, take it as a sign that it is time to invest in yourself and your goals. Angel Number 1010 means that you are working towards fulfilling your ultimate spiritual purpose in life.

Angel Number 1111

Angel Number 1111 is a highly spiritual number that speaks directly to your intuition. This rare number appears in your life as a sign that the powers that be, are blessing you. Take Angel Number 1111 as a sign of opportunity.

Angel Number 1212

This Angel Number signifies duality; specifically, the duality between the self and the divine. Angel Number 1212 represents you and your spirit guides working together for your ultimate destiny. When the number 1212 appears to you, take it as a sign to keep focused on your path, and remember that you have the help of the angels above you.

Angel Number 1234

This Angel Number includes the first four single digits in sequence, representing progress and movement forward. This divine number speaks to your progress on your life's path. When Angel Number 1234 appears in your life, take it as a sign that you are on the right course.

Chapter Eight: The Life Path Number

Your Life Path Number, which is calculated from your date of birth, is perhaps the most important number in your numerology chart, and it is often the first one any new practitioner of numerology will calculate. It is equivalent to the sun sign in astrology, as it tells you about your core self. Your Life Path Number can tell you about your true purpose in life, as well as your individual strengths and weaknesses.

Your Life Path Number, put simply, represents the road you travel in life. This number reveals to you both the opportunities and the challenges you will find along the way.

Calculate Your Life Path Number

To calculate your Life Path Number, you will simply sum the digits in your day of birth, then sum the digits in your month of birth, then sum the digits in your year of birth, and break all of these down to single digit numbers. Then, sum these numbers together and break them down to a single digit one final time. This is called the root number. For example:

August 28, 1942

August = 8

$28 = 2+8 = 10 = 1+0 = 1$

$1942 = 1+9+4+2 = 16 = 1+6 = 7$

$8+1+7 = 16 = 1+6 = 7$

So, a person who is born on August 28, 1943 has a Life Path Number of 8. Another example:

January 4, 1995

January = 1

4 = 4

1995 = 1+9+9+5 = 24 = 2+4 = 6

1+4+6 = 11

Because 11 is a Master Number, we do not continue to break this number down into single digits. Instead, we say that someone who was born on January 4, 1995 has a Life Path Number of 11, which is rare and special—more on that later.

Life Path Number 1

Those with a Life Path Number of 1 are natural born leaders who assume responsibility to provide for and protect their loved ones. If you have a Life Path Number of 1, you have a great amount of determination and drive to get results. Once you are committed to a goal, you will not let anything, or anyone stand in your way of achieving it.

A powerful force, your Life Path Number 1 commands respect and attention. On the flip side, you can be quick to anger when things don't go your way, as your natural born leadership gives you a touch of a controlling nature. You like to be in command of important work and do not like playing a supportive role, but rather prefer the limelight. You can be overly critical of both your own shortcomings and those of others, demanding perfection.

Those with a Life Path Number of 1 are destined to be successful in life, provided they apply their determination and drive properly. When it comes to business and work, you shine when you are your own boss;

Life Path Number 1's make excellent business owners and entrepreneurs. Life Path Number 1, though, has a tendency toward conceit. Take care not to become too concerned with appearances.

Life Path Number 2

If you have a Life Path Number of 2, you are a very sensitive person. This quality is both a strength and a weakness depending on how you harness it. On the one hand, you are able to experience life to a deep level that others do not, but on the other, you have a tendency to hold back for fear of being hurt by others.

Along with your sensitivity, your Life Path Number of 2 brings a great deal of perceptiveness. You are keenly in tune with the feelings of others—and empathic. You work well with others and tend to be the peacemaker of the group, helping to keep everyone together and working in harmony. Life Path Number 2 does not work in the limelight, but is often a powerful player behind the scenes. In personal relationships, you are an attentive lover and friend. People feel drawn to you and love to be around your peaceful nature.

However, if your Life Path Number is 2, your sensitivity makes your ego rather delicate and quick to bruise. If you do not take the inherent risk involved in opening your true self up to others, you will, in turn, build resentment and tend to run from conflict.

Life Path Number 3

Life Path Number 3 is all about expression and creativity. These individuals are some of the greatest artists, musicians, and poets. In order to hone your innate gift of self-expression, you will need to commit to the hard work of study and practice. Take care to practice focus and discipline, lest you squander your talents.

If your Life Path Number is 3, you are the life of the party! You have a gift for making friends and love to be the center of attention; a social butterfly. You inspire everyone you meet with your sunny disposition, and your optimism, in the face of setbacks, helps you overcome any challenge that comes your way in life.

The dark side of Life Path Number 3 is that you can be irresponsible with money due to your disorganized nature. You are also vulnerable to criticism and surprisingly sensitive; when someone hurts you, you tend to either withdraw or pretend like it never happened and come back with a joke. You must learn not to cover up your true feelings with humor.

Life Path Number 4

Those with a Life Path Number of 4 are "salt of the earth" types: hardworking, dedicated, practical, and down to earth. If your Life Path Number is 4, you will tend to be very organized, to appreciate order, and to have strong convictions about what you believe to be right and wrong.

With a Life Path Number of 4, you are destined for success, but only after putting in a lot of hard work to get there. You possess a level of dedication that far outshines those around you and need to be careful not to come off as bossy and mean; try not to judge these other Life Path Numbers too harshly.

Life Path Number 4 makes you very methodical and meticulous. You are good with money and value financial stability, however you can easily become too rigid and resistant to change. You should try to cultivate some flexibility in your personality. If you are too cautious and resist change, you can miss out on great opportunities in life.

Life Path Number 5

Life Path Number 5 is all about freedom. Those with this Life Path Number value their freedom above all else. They are lovers of travel and great adventure. This love is destined to take Life Path Number 5 on a journey through life, meeting many new people and seeing many new things. This in turn broadens Number 5's horizons; these people tend to be very open minded and accepting of others who are different from them.

If your Life Path Number is 5, you are one of those rare people who actually like and do well with change. You adapt expertly to any curveball life throws your way! An excellent communicator, you will do well in a career that uses your personality, such as sales or politics. You may also be strongly compelled by the idea of being your own boss.

However, your love of freedom makes you hesitant to commit, be it in relationships or in work. You lack discipline and order, and your zest for life, if unchecked, can easily lead to substance abuse or other addiction issues. Your challenge with the Life Path Number 5 is to cultivate focus and commitment in your endeavors, lest all your great ideas never see the light of day.

Life Path Number 6

Those with the Life Path Number 6 are said to be the caretakers of the world. They are endowed with a great deal of compassion for others and live a life of service. If your Life Path Number is 6, you are a natural healer and the type of person that others turn to for comfort. You tend to take on the responsibility of caring for those close to you. At times, this can make you feel overburdened. One of your challenges in life is to learn when to say no.

With a Life Path Number of 6, you are often admired and adored by others, but yet you remain very humble. You make an excellent friend and an even better romantic partner and parent, because you are generous, caring, and giving—as well as charismatic and charming.

These individuals tend to be very creative and talented while also possessing a flair for business due to their charm. What you need to look out for is who you choose to spend your time with and give your love and caring to. Life Path Number 6 is at risk for attracting abusive partners who take advantage of your love and generosity.

Life Path Number 7

Life Path Number 7 is the seeker. Those with this Life Path Number are deeply spiritual people who are drawn to finding the answers behind the mysteries of life. While Life Path Number 7 is incredibly spiritual, these individuals also possess a keen mind and well-developed rationality. They are capable of superior analytical thought and tend to thrive when solving puzzles of all kinds.

If your Life Path Number is 7, you are likely an introvert or a lone wolf. You prefer to do your thinking alone, uninterrupted by outside influence. Your privacy and autonomy are deeply important to you and, as such, it can be challenging for you to make and maintain intimate relationships. You are extremely careful to guard your rich inner life from others and do not open up easily.

Those with the Life Path Number of 7 must be careful not to withdraw too much into isolation, which can breed loneliness. This loneliness can then even morph into jealousy and resentment. Take care to nourish your relationships so that you can live up to the full potential of this very special Life Path Number.

Life Path Number 8

Those with a Life Path Number of 8 are destined for success in business and finance! These individuals are natural leaders with a talent for management, not only in work but in personal matters, as well. More than any other life path, Life Path Number 8 has the potential for fabulous wealth and financial success, but this comes with a higher potential for downfall, as well.

If your Life Path Number is 8, you must be very careful to avoid succumbing to greed and a lust for power. Your challenge in life is to learn that the real value of money and success lies in what you can share with others. You must, in short, use your powers for good rather than for evil. Your Life Path Number 8 talents are only fully realized when you use them for the good of all mankind.

Those with a Life Path Number of 8 are also prone to living beyond their means, as their keen sense of style and love of comfort and lavishness can lead them to overspending. But Life Path Number 8 is also a loving family member and a cherished and generous friend. You attract good people into your life.

Life Path Number 9

If you have a Life Path Number of 9, you are a true humanitarian and philanthropist. Your deep love for the world leads you to try everything within your power to make the world a better place. You have an innate need to sacrifice, to give your time, energy, and money to a greater good, and you find your fulfillment and satisfaction in the giving of yourself.

Individuals with a Life Path Number of 9 tend to be very unbiased when it comes to judging other people, and in fact these people attract others from all walks of life due to their magnetic personalities. In addition to your egalitarian ideals, your Life Path Number of 9 grants you a great deal of imagination and creativity, as well as the gift of seeing the beauty in everything.

The dark side of Life Path Number 9, though, is that you tend to be disappointed easily when things don't line up with your expectations. Thus, because you are an idealist, you can become easily frustrated with the state of the world. Take care to appreciate how far you and others have come, rather than to constantly be pushing yourself and everyone else to the next level.

Life Path Number 11

Master Number 11 imparts a great deal of potential as a Life Path Number, but it also comes with significant challenges. If your Life Path Number is Master Number 11, you are a supremely intuitive person with a supercharged psychic energy. This energy flows through you and makes you an inspiration to others. But, if you do not learn to harness it, this energy can cause you inner turmoil and wreak havoc on your emotional wellbeing.

The truth of your intuitive gifts is that you are a channel between the spirit realm and the earthly realm. Great insight is available to you with little work or effort on your part; it just seems to come naturally. Your destiny with a Life Path Number of 11 is to be a righteous healer and peacemaker in the world, using your intuitive gifts to spread a divine message to others.

However, the intuitive power of Master Number 11 is a double-edged sword, and people with this Life Path Number tend to be highly self-critical and can become paralyzed by self-doubt. You may be challenged in your life with depression and a lack of confidence. This confidence is the key to finding and using your true, complete potential to change the world.

Life Path Number 22

If your Life Path Number is Master Number 22, you are destined to be a master builder. You were born under one of the most powerful possible Life Path Numbers, but this power comes with additional challenges due to having Master Number 22 in your numerology chart. Because your power is based on your inner vision and strong ideals, this is a somewhat delicate form of power.

In order to harness this power to its full potential, you must learn to accept and love the dualities within yourself, as your idealism fights with your sense of practicality. You must learn to be, at once, a visionary and to keep your feet on the ground. This is the true potential of the master builder, Life Path Number 22.

If your Life Path Number is 22, you tend to be focused more on your work and your dreams than on personal relationships. In intimate relationships, you must be careful not to become controlling or manipulative. Keep the ultimate goal of your higher purpose in sight to guide you.

Life Path Number 33

It is extremely rare to have a Life Path Number of 33. Those with this Master Number for their Life Path Number have the potential to be the master teachers of the world; however, because 33 is a Master Number, this potential comes with a unique set of challenges. If your Life Path Number is 33, your divine potential lies in your ability to guide others.

With this life path number, you have access to a great amount of spiritual knowledge. Your talent is your ability to go inward and use your intuition to gain this knowledge and share it with others. Along with your keen intuition comes a sincere compassion for others. This caring nature leads you to take on responsibility for others—even when you should perhaps not. Your challenge with a Life Path Number of 33 is to find the balance between giving and being walked on.

Life Path Number 33 finds itself attracted to weaker people—these individuals tend to think they can "fix" their partners. For this reason, those with the Life Path Number of 33 are at risk of being in abusive relationships with others who will take advantage of their generosity.

Chapter Nine: The Destiny Number

In contrast to your Life Path Number, which is based on your date of birth, your Destiny Number is calculated based on your full name. If the Life Path Number tells you what your greater purpose in life is, then your Destiny Number tells you how you will go about accomplishing this. For this reason, the Destiny Number is sometimes also called the Expression Number: It is about how you express yourself! Your Destiny Number, when analyzed alongside your Life Path Number as two of the most important calculations in your numerology chart, can provide a nuanced interpretation of your numerological chart.

Calculate Your Destiny Number

Traditionally birth names are used to calculate the Destiny Number, but some numerologists believe that you can, in fact, change your Destiny Number by changing your name. Recall that Pythagoras taught his students that each letter of the alphabet is said to correspond to a number 1-9:

1. A, J, S
2. B, K, T
3. C, L, U
4. D, M, V
5. E, N, W
6. F, O, X
7. G, P, Y
8. H, Q, Z
9. I, R

To calculate your Destiny Number, you will use the numbers-to-letters chart above to convert the letters in your first, middle, and last names to numbers. Then sum these numbers individually and reduce to a single digit, and finally sum these single digits together and then reduce again if necessary. For example:

Mary Ann Rose

Mary = 4+1+9+7 = 21 = 2+1 = 3

Ann = 1+5+5 = 11 = 1+1 = 2

Rose = 9+6+1+5 = 21 = 2+1 = 3

3+2+3 = 8

So, an individual named Mary Ann Rose has a Destiny Number of 8. Another example:

Jonathan Brian Green

Jonathan = 1+6+5+1+2+8+1+5 = 29 = 2+9 = 11 (Remember that we do not break Master Numbers down into their Root Numbers!)

Brian = 2+9+9+1+5 = 26 = 2+6 = 8

Green = 7+9+5+5+5 = 21 = 2+1 = 3

11 + 8 + 3 = 22

So, Jonathan Brian Greene has a Destiny Number of 22, which is a Master Number.

Destiny Number 1

Those with a Destiny Number of 1 are natural born leaders and independent individualists. If your Destiny Number is 1, you are an original and very ambitious person with a ton of courage. You love to explore and innovate. Confident and energetic, you can become easily frustrated when you feel limited by other people's ideas.

Destiny Number 2

If you have a Destiny Number of 2, your talent is working well with others tactfully. Your excellent sense of intuition makes you in tune with other people's personalities in different situations, which helps you to act subtly and tactfully. With this Destiny Number, you possess diplomatic talents. You bring out the best in others.

Destiny Number 3

With a Destiny Number of 3, you are outgoing, expressive, and possess boundless optimism. You're a cheerful and inspiring person; you attract others to you with your great charm. If your Destiny Number is 3, you are a supremely creative individual and an excellent communicator. You would do well in the arts or writing.

Destiny Number 4

Those with a Destiny Number of 4 are the foundation of their communities, the bedrock of society. If your Destiny Number is 4, you are well suited to management, as you are a methodical organizer and systematic thinker. What's more, you are very capable and hardworking, and you have the means to accomplish anything you put your mind to.

Destiny Number 5

Those who have a 5 for their Destiny Number are free spirited adventurers and lovers of excitement. If your Destiny Number is 5, you are the kind of person who is extremely attracted to freedom—so much so—that you would do anything to protect your freedom. You need to be free in order to be true to yourself. You have a destiny to travel.

Destiny Number 6

A Destiny Number of 6 is said to make a person loving and caring. Those with this Destiny Number tend to be the type to put their loved ones first ahead of their own needs. If 6 is your Destiny Number, you are a trustworthy and honest friend, and others see you as being responsible as well as extremely helpful.

Destiny Number 7

Destiny Number 7 is gifted with a keen mind for analytics and a hunger to answer life's greatest questions. If your Destiny Number is 7, you are very interested in learning and would do well to explore science, philosophy, and mysticism. Your ultimate destiny is the pursuit of truth, which you have all the capabilities needed to uncover.

Destiny Number 8

Those with a Destiny Number of 8 are destined to achieve greatness. These individuals will work hard and put their talents to use, becoming the best and most successful at anything they put their minds to. If you have a Destiny Number of 8, you are a very competitive person who enjoys a challenge. You are likely to make a lot of money in your lifetime.

Destiny Number 9

If you have a Destiny Number of 9, you have a great humanitarian spirit. Your high ideals and love for others attract you to humanitarian causes, and you are willing to fight to make the world a better place. This Destiny Number represents the ultimate idealist whose destiny is to be the righter of wrongs and to transform the world altogether with your vision.

Destiny Number 11

If your Destiny Number is Master Number 11, you are a highly psychically charged person who attracts powerful visions and enlightenment. You have a powerful presence, and you may not even realize what kind of power you have. With a Destiny Number of 11, you are a channel through which divinity flows into the mortal world.

Destiny Number 22

If your Destiny Number is Master Number 22, you are a big dreamer with far-reaching goals that are enormous in their scope. Your destiny is to change history, leaving your mark on the world. You are capable of anything you put your mind to, and that includes turning your wildest ideas into reality. This Destiny Number imparts on you a great potential for accomplishment.

Destiny Number 33

It is extremely rare to have a Destiny Number of 33, and all of the traits of Master Number 33 are amplified. Those with this Master Number for their Destiny Number are extremely kind, caring, and generous people. If your Destiny Number is 33, you have a great level of creativity and self-expression in addition to your well-beloved kindness. Your destiny is to teach something important to the world.

Chapter Ten: The Soul Urge Number

The third important number on your numerological chart that we will cover is called your Soul Urge Number, or sometimes simply Soul Number or the Heart's Desire Number. This number reveals the deeper, inner you and tells you what your greatest desires are. The Soul Urge Number is all about who you really are deep down inside.

While knowing your Life Path Number tells you about your greatest purpose in life, adding the understanding of your Soul Urge Number ensures that you will gain a better knowledge of who you are authentically. Knowing what your soul's greatest wishes are will help bring you peace of mind, as you can then use your talents and skills (as divined by your Life Path and Destiny Numbers) to make your heart's desires come true!

Calculate Your Soul Urge Number

Like your Destiny Number, your Soul Urge Number is calculated using your name—however, in this case, you are only using the vowels. It is said that consonants represent your public, outward persona, while vowels represent your innermost feelings, beliefs and traits. So essentially, the vowels of your name represent your soul!

The values of the vowels are as follows:

- A = 1
- E = 5
- I = 9
- O = 6
- U = 3
- Y = 7

It is important to note that you will only include the letter Y or the number 7 in your calculations if the Y in your name is used as a vowel. For example, with the name Emily, we count the Y for the soul urge calculation:

Emily = E+I+Y = 5+9+7 = 21 = 2+1 = 3

However, in the case of the name Yancy, the first Y acts as a consonant, so it is not used when calculating the Soul Urge Number. Only the second Y, which acts as a vowel, is counted:

Yancy = A+Y = 1+7 = 8

Note that when a word that ends in another vowel + the letter Y, the Y usually is not counted because it is not adding any additional vowel sound. Take for example the name Finlay:

Finlay = I+A = 9+1 = 10 = 1+0 = 1

One trick to knowing whether to count the Y in a name is to count the number of syllables. You should only have as many letters/numbers in your Soul Urge Number calculation as there are syllables in your name.

Soul Urge Number 1

Those with a Soul Urge Number of 1 have an overpowering need to remain independent. If your Soul Urge Number is 1, you dream of being the leader in your field, and you have the confidence and courage necessary to lead.

Soul Urge Number 2

If you have a Soul Urge Number of 2, you have a deep desire to devote your life to loving someone else; you make an excellent partner or spouse. You are a very emotional, gentle, and even sensitive person—this stems from your powerful intuition.

Soul Urge Number 3

If you have a Soul Urge Number of 3, your heart's desire is to have a good time while you're on this planet! You are a friendly, outgoing person who easily makes new companions. With this Soul Urge Number, you are gifted with self-expression and would make a great artist or writer.

Soul Urge Number 4

Those with a Soul Urge Number of 4 place a great deal of value on a stable home and family life. If your Soul Urge Number is 4, you are likely to despise sudden change and prefer order and neatness in your life. Soul Urge Number 4 is nothing if not dependable and supportive of their loved ones.

Soul Urge Number 5

Those who have a 5 for their Soul Urge Number are adventurers with a great love of travel. Very flexible and able to adapt effortlessly to changes in your environment, your Soul Urge Number of 5 means that deep down, you seek freedom more than anything else in life.

Soul Urge Number 6

A Soul Urge Number of 6 is said to represent individuals whose greatest happiness is found in sharing love with others. If your Soul Urge Number is 6, you are likely a giving, caring person who others turn to for help, and you keep a comfortable home where you love to invite in guests.

Soul Urge Number 7

Soul Urge Number 7 values mental ability and knowledge over all else. Those with this Soul Urge Number are destined to unravel the mysteries of life. If you have a Soul Urge Number of 7, you are an exceptionally smart person who seeks the truth in all things.

Soul Urge Number 8

Those with a Soul Urge Number of 8 have great ambitions, and their deepest desire is for power, wealth, and success. If you have a Soul Urge Number of 8, you are a visionary leader, and you have the necessary talents to bring about the vast success you seek.

Soul Urge Number 9

If you have a Soul Urge Number of 9, your greatest satisfaction and fulfillment in life comes from knowing that you have been of service to others. You are a perfectionist with high ideals. With a Soul Urge Number of 9, you are destined to leave the world better than you found it.

Soul Urge Number 11

If your Soul Urge Number is Master Number 11, you are wise beyond your years and deeply intuitive. Your greatest drive in life is to find and maintain harmony and balance. With this Soul Urge Number, you sincerely dislike and avoid conflict.

Soul Urge Number 22

If your Soul Urge Number is Master Number 22, your deepest desire is to make a creation that will make the world a better place. You have a strong drive to manifest vision into reality. With this Soul Urge Number, you are both inventive and down-to-earth; you are capable of making all your dreams come true.

Soul Urge Number 33

It is extremely rare to have a Soul Urge Number of 33. Those with this Master Number for their Soul Urge Number are committed to caring for their loved ones. If this is your Soul Urge Number, you are happiest and most fulfilled when with your family and friends. You are deeply loyal and never let down a friend.

Chapter Eleven: The Personality Number

The next important number on your numerological chart that we will cover is called your Personality Number, also sometimes called your Outer Personality Number. Your Personality Number tells you about how other people see you. This number reveals the outer you, what you give out to the world—or put simply, your personality!

Calculate Your Personality Number

In contrast to your Soul Urge Number, which as you recall speaks to your innermost desires and is calculated based on only the vowels in your name, your Personality Number is calculated using only the consonants. As you learned in the previous chapter, consonants represent your public, outward persona, while vowels represent your innermost feelings, beliefs and traits. So, it makes sense that your personality number comes from the consonants in your name.

You can actually calculate two different Personality Numbers: One by using your full birth name, which is your true Personality Number, and one using your nickname, which is your minor Personality Number. This second number has less of an influence on you and your numerological chart, but it can help lend a nuanced understanding to who you are as a person.

The values of the consonants are as follows:

1. J, S
2. B, K, T
3. C, L
4. D, M, V
5. N, W
6. F, X

7. G, P, Y
8. H, Q, Z
9. R

Remember to only count the letter Y as a number 7 in your Personality Number calculation if it is used as a consonant in the name. For example:

Yancy = Y+N+C = 7+5+3 = 15 = 1+5 = 6

In Yancy's name, we count the first Y because it acts as a consonant, but we do not count the Y at the end of the name because this Y is acting as a vowel.

Personality Number 1

Those with a Personality Number of 1 appear controlled and capable to others. These personality types are courageous and place a high value on determination in the face of challenges. If your Personality Number is 1, you radiate outwardly with a dynamic energy that can be intimidating to others. You might try to soften yourself a bit and be careful of coming off as aggressive.

Personality Number 2

If you have a Personality Number of 2, you come across to others as approachable and friendly. People tend to think of you as a safe person they can trust. However, this same quality that attracts others to you also makes you sensitive. With a Personality Number of 2, you are likely to have experienced some hurt or trauma in your past that keeps you from fully opening up to people today. It is a good idea to work on healing your wounds and overcoming your shyness.

Personality Number 3

Personality Number 3 is full of life. If this is your Personality Number, others see you as charming, inspiring, and uplifting. You are a popular person, the life of any party, and other people love to be around you because you are fun! However, the downside to the Number 3 personality type is that you can be flighty and irresponsible, and flippant when it comes to keeping your commitments.

Personality Number 4

Those with a Personality Number of 4 are family-oriented people who are good providers and protectors. If your Personality Number is 4, others see you as dependable and honest; you are the glue that holds a community together. People tend to trust your judgement and come to you for advice. With a Personality Number of 4, you present yourself as someone who is very particular and precise; however, you are in danger of appearing controlling if you do not reign these qualities of your personality in.

Personality Number 5

Those who have a 5 for their Personality Number are seen by others as bright and innovative people. If your Personality Number is 5, it is likely that other people love to talk to you and spend time around you. Upbeat and optimistic, you are a supremely adventurous spirit and are highly adaptable to whatever situation you end up in. However, the dark side of this personality type is that you may indulge too much in your urges, which can lead to an addictive personality.

Personality Number 6

Those with a Personality Number of 6 radiate outwardly a sense of compassion. If your Personality Number is 6, other people readily sense your warmth and think of you as a good person; the kind of person they can go to for help with their problems. Because of this, Number 6 personality types should be on guard against being taken advantage of. With this Personality Number, your penchant for service puts you at risk of martyring yourself if taken to the extreme.

Personality Number 7

If you have a Personality Number of 7, others see you as mysterious and a little bit otherworldly; however, this mysterious quality tends to draw people to you. With this Personality Number, you are well respected for your intellect and wit, but people are likely to see you as cold and withdrawn. Because you are so intelligent, your Personality Number of 7 puts you at risk of coming off as an arrogant know-it-all.

Personality Number 8

Those with a Personality Number of 8 appear outwardly to others as very strong and powerful individuals. If this is your Personality Number, you can be an intimidating force due to your natural authority. You radiate confidence, and people respect and look up to you for guidance. The weakness of Personality Number 8 is their tendency toward conceit and greed. You must remember to be generous with others and share your gifts with the world, lest you become authoritarian in your leadership.

Personality Number 9

If you have a Personality Number of 9, you appear to others to be elegant and well put-together—downright aristocratic at times. These personality types are in complete control of the image they put out into the world. Your Personality Number of 9 grants you grace, elegance, and charisma; but while many admire you, you also have a tendency toward arrogance. Take care not to think of yourself as separate from or above the rest of the world, lest you become aloof.

Personality Number 11

If your Personality Number is Master Number 11, it is likely that you have overcome the shyness and inhibition that held you back earlier in life. Now, others see you as confident and self-assured, but you retain the innocent sensitivity that you were born with. People tend to see those with Personality Number 11 as gentle, caring individuals. People love to be around you because you make others feel loved. However, you must guard against being taken advantage of throughout your life.

Personality Number 22

If your Personality Number is Master Number 22, you appear to others as reliable and consistent. Other people tend to trust you and seek your judgement. With this personality type, you are likely to be a pillar of your community, and other people rely on you to do your job as well as you do. However, you should be careful not to become deluded into thinking you are beyond questioning, lest you become controlling and power-hungry.

Personality Number 33

It is extremely rare to have a Personality Number of 33. Those with this Master Number for their Personality Number inspire confidence in others, who will often want to unburden themselves on you. If your Personality Number is 33, you have a big influence on your community and the potential to do something great in the world. However, you are not a very good judge of character, and you tend to always see the best in people, even when they are out to hurt you.

Chapter Twelve: The Birth Day Number

The last of the Core Numbers in your numerology chart and the Core Number with the least influence: Your Birth Day Number tells you what unique attributes you have to offer. In short, your Birth Day Number represents your gift to the world!

Calculate Your Birth Day Number

You don't actually have to calculate your Birth Day Number at all! This one is easy: Simply, take the number of the day of the month on which you were born. That's it. Unlike with the other core numbers, numerologists do not break the Birth Day Number down into its Root Number.

For example, if you were born on December 1st, 1954, your Birth Day Number is 1. If you were born on April 30th, 1995, your Birth Day Number is 30. It really is that simple! Read on to find out what your birthday number has to say about your special gifts.

Birth Day Number 1

If you were born on the 1st day of the month, your Birth Day Number is 1, making you an innovative self-starter. You possess a powerful determination of will and can conquer any challenge that comes your way. You are never afraid to be the first at something and love to try new things.

Birth Day Number 2

If you were born on the 2nd day of the month, your Birth Day Number is 2, making you an intuitive person with a talent for finding solutions. You are unbiased and therefore able to see all sides of the situation, making you an excellent source of advice for others.

Birth Day Number 3

If you were born on the 3rd day of the month, your Birth Day Number is 3, and self-expression comes naturally to you. You're an excellent communicator and a great conversationalist. You have a talent for art, be it visual, musical, or otherwise, and your shining personality is an inspiration to all those around you.

Birth Day Number 4

Those with a Birth Day Number of 4 are rock solid, stable and rational. You work hard and can persevere through any obstacle. You are a dependable friend and other people love to be around you.

Birth Day Number 5

If you were born on the 5th day of the month your Birth Day Number is 5, endowing you with the rare gift of adaptability. Because you love the excitement of change, you are prepared to take on any curveball life throws at you.

Birth Day Number 6

A Birth Day Number of 6 means that you are a natural nurturer with a big heart. You love to help others and facilitate healing, and you fiercely protect those close to you. Your gift to the world is your love!

Birth Day Number 7

Birth Day Number 7 is said to possess a keen and curious mind. Your gift is your ability to learn, not just in the earthly realm, but in the spiritual.

Birth Day Number 8

Those with a Birth Day Number of 8 are destined for success! If your Birth Day Number is 8, you have a gift for reaching all of the goals you set. You are very capable and powerful to match your exceptional ambition.

Birth Day Number 9

If you have a Birth Day Number of 9, you are a supremely compassionate person with a heart of gold. You find your fulfillment in life by helping others. Your gift is that you are divinely destined to change the world for the better through your acts of service.

Birth Day Number 10

Birth Day Number 10 is a natural born leader. If this is your Birth Day Number, you have a sharp mind—your gift is that you not only can imagine fantastic new solutions, but also organize all the details necessary to carry out your plans.

Birth Day Number 11

Birth Day Number 11 represents great insight. If this is your Birth Day Number, you have a keen perception and tend to be well aware of what surrounds you. Your gift is your strong intuition, which helps you understand and guide others.

Birth Day Number 12

Birth Day Number 12 is said to bestow gifts of creativity and imagination. If your Birth Day Number is 10, you have a great way of expressing yourself. You are a unique person who shines brightly and inspires others.

Birth Day Number 13

If you have a Birth Day Number of 13, you are a hard worker. Your gift is an optimistic yet practical way of seeing the world, which helps you stay on track toward reaching your high ideals.

Birth Day Number 14

Those who have a 14 for their Birth Day Number are very open minded individuals who love to try new things. However, if this is your Birth Day Number, you are also blessed with practicality. Your pragmatism will help you go far.

Birth Day Number 15

If your Birth Day Number is 15, you have a deep capacity for loving others. You are curious and a social butterfly. You will meet a lot of different people in your life, all of whom you will touch with your gift of warmth.

Birth Day Number 16

If 16 is your Birth Day Number, you are a very inquisitive soul, always determined to get to the truth. You have an uncanny ability to read other people's minds. If your Birth Day Number is 16, your gift to the world is your wisdom.

Birth Day Number 17

If you have a Birth Day Number of 17, you are a self-starter who prefers to work alone, and you accomplish incredible things when left to your own devices. Your independence and ambition are your gifts that help you to build the skills you will gain in life.

Birth Day Number 18

If your Birth Day Number is 18, you are an open hearted person who wants to do good for the world. You may be shy and prefer to remain independent, but your true gift to the world is your capacity for service to others. With a Birth Day Number of 18, you are destined to leave the world better than you found it.

Birth Day Number 19

Those who have a 19 for their Birth Day Number are all about independence and being self-sufficient. If this is your Birth Day Number, you are a courageous risk-taker who brings great things into your life. Your gift is your great level of capability.

Birth Day Number 20

If you have a Birth Day Number of 20, your gift is that you relate to other people on a deep, almost cosmic level. You have a skill for making relationships harmonious and cooperative when you are involved.

Birth Day Number 21

If your Birth Day Number is 21, you are an outgoing person who thrives in social situations. With this Birth Day Number, you feel fulfilled when you connect with others. Your gift is your natural charm, which along with your communication skills makes you an excellent person to know.

Birth Day Number 22

If you were born on the 22nd day of the month, your Birth Day Number is Master Number 22. Those who have a 22 for their Birth Day Number are destined to make something great. If this is your Birth Day Number, you are a hard worker and you get along well with others on a team.

Birth Day Number 23

Those who have a Birth Day Number of 23 are said to have a great zest for life. If this is your Birth Day Number, you love to explore and experience new things. You have an easygoing nature, and your gift to others is your inspiring optimism.

Birth Day Number 24

If your Birth Day Number is 24, you have a heart of gold. Your gift to the world is your loyal heart. Those with this Birth Day Number are nurturers and providers who are very good at maintaining healthy, balanced relationships.

Birth Day Number 25

Those with a Birth Day Number of 25 are very curious individuals who take in and process much information, both consciously and subconsciously. If this is your Birth Day Number, your gift to the world is your desire for knowledge, which will allow you to serve others and take you to great places.

Birth Day Number 26

Birth Day Number 26 is said to impart a strong drive for success, however, if this is your Birth Day Number, you will feel most fulfilled when your work benefits others and not just yourself. You have an intuitive gift for understanding what other people want, so you are able to solve problems and meet needs seemingly effortlessly.

Birth Day Number 27

Those with a Birth Day Number of 27 are very open-minded, compassionate, and tolerant to others. If this is your Birth Day Number, you have a gift for taking in huge amounts of knowledge, which you are destined to apply toward a higher good.

Birth Day Number 28

If you have a Birth Day Number of 28, you understand the value of working with others and make a great team member and leader. Your gift in life is your ability to drive your team forward and make them succeed. With this birthday number, you are destined to be a compassionate leader.

Birth Day Number 29

If your Birth Day Number is 29, you have a gift for bringing everything together. Your powerful intuition brings your subconscious insight, allowing you to see, clearly, the connectivity between everyone and everything!

Birth Day Number 30

If your Birth Day Number is 30, you are an original thinker with innovative ideas. Your gift to the world is your creativity, which you use to convey your great ideas. With a Birth Day Number of 30, you are destined to uplift others.

Birth Day Number 31

Those with 31 for their Birth Day Number have a balanced approach to life, mixing imagination in equal parts with practicality. If this is your Birth Day Number, your dual gifts are your creativity and the necessary organizational skills to manifest your dreams.

Final Words

Now, we have peeled back the shroud of mystery surrounding the vibrational frequency of numbers. You know what each common number means and how to calculate all of your Core Numbers. You are well on your way to creating your own numerological chart!

Keep studying and seek out additional resources to broaden and deepen your understanding of numerology and how it relates to your life. A deeper knowledge of who you are as a person and what you can expect out of life is waiting for you to uncover it.